Samantha Edwards

REWRITNG THE HOLLYWOOD RULEBOOK: THE MELISSA MCCARTHY STORY

The Biography of A Beautiful Misfit's Champion

Copyright © 2024 by Samantha Edwards

All rights reserved. No part of this publication may be reproduced, stored or transmitted in any form or by any means, electronic, mechanical, photocopying, recording, scanning, or otherwise without written permission from the publisher. It is illegal to copy this book, post it to a website, or distribute it by any other means without permission.

First edition

This book was professionally typeset on Reedsy
Find out more at reedsy.com

Contents

Preface 1
1. Early Life & Education 5
2. Early Comedy Career 10
3. Television Breakthrough 14
4. Film Fame Begins 18
5. Movie Stardom 22
6. Dramatic Projects and Acclaim 26
7. Production Roles and Business Ventures 31
8. Awards and Achievements 37
9. Balancing Career and Family 42
10. Continued Prominence and Impact 48
Conclusion 54
Afterword 59

   1.

   2.

   3.

   4.

   5.

   6.

   7.

   8.

9.
10.
11.
12.

Preface

INTRODUCTION

Melissa McCarthy: A Comedic Icon

From her humble beginnings in Illinois all the way to dominating Hollywood movie screens, Melissa McCarthy has risen become one of the most popular, famous and influential comedic actresses of her generation through consistent hard work, undeniable talent, and sheer determination even in the face of sexism, discrimination and rejection. This biography tells the improbable story of how an awkward, "loud" and overweight young girl who struggled to fit societal beauty standards transformed herself into a revered performer, role model and advocate.

The preface traces the arc of Melissa's journey. Growing up, she battled anxieties during what was an otherwise typical upbringing in middle America. As a bright and eager young woman she overcame initial skepticism to attend the prestigious Staircase theater school at Joliet Catholic Academy. Her passion for performance spurred McCarthy to relocate alone at age 18 to the cutthroat environment of New

York City to pursue her dreams of stardom. After difficult first months juggling odd jobs just to subsist and being confronted with rampant sexism as a women in comedy, she persevered to gain admittance to the iconic improvisational comedy troupe The Groundlings that served as the launchpad for numerous famous stars over the prior decades.

However, success was not immediate. Melissa spent almost a decade slowly building a reputation on the LA comedy circuit through standup appearances and sporadic TV guest roles despite limited early opportunities to shine on screen. Her big break finally came when she was cast as the endearing and quirky chef Sookie St. James on the fast-rising comedy-drama series Gilmore Girls in 2000. The first stage was set for Melissa to display her natural humor and expressiveness to a growing mainstream audience through Gilmore Girls' 7 seasons until leaving in 2007. With her talent validated and with growing credentials, she continued receive more prominent parts such as her Emmy-nominated turn as the lead character Molly on the sitcom Mike & Molly.

In 2011, Melissa's comedic skills exploded onto the global stage with her iconic, riotous and scene-stealing performance as the outspoken Megan Price in Bridesmaids. This landmark role represented a culmination of her 20 years of trials and tribulations to cement herself as undeniable star in

Hollywood on her own terms. Though typecast early in her career due to appearance, Bridesmaids underscored that McCarthy exceeded cookie cutter expectations of beauty with a blockbuster success celebrated equally for its both actress' humor as well as a groundbreaking script focusing on complex women. From that launching pad, McCarthy unleashed an unprecedented run headlining major commercial comedies one after another including Identity Thief, The Heat, Tammy, Spy while also diversifying into family films, action adventures, and children's animation. Each outing brought unprecedented feats like becoming the first woman to lead a movie past $35 million opening weekend (The Heat) all the while earning over $650 million in box office just in the first 2 years post-Bridesmaids.

Yet behind the fame and fortune, Melissa has never lost her humble, candid persona from early days despite ongoing barriers for plus-size actresses. She leveraged popularity to empower women of all shapes and looks by launching her inclusive fashion label Seven7, advocating for body positivity, producing female-led projects, and becoming an inspiration to millions. Time Magazine named her one of the 100 most influential people in the world in 2016. After overcoming stereotypes to redefine comedic stardom at midlife when most actresses struggle for substantive roles, Melissa gathered acclaim for more nuanced dramatic turns in awards contenders like Can You Ever Forgive Me alongside recent blockbuster endeavors. She forayed into writing/production all while balancing devoted family life with husband.

Now entering her 50s with fortune beyond imagination at birth having risen from obscurity into permanent pop culture stardom through authentic humor and resilience, Melissa McCarthy's remarkable biography will explore the key inflection points, colorful roles and fearless decisions which allowed this self-made, underestimated woman to ascend the absolute apex of entertainment success as a complete multimedia force cementing legendary status that endures generations. The subsequent chapters will delve into fascinating specifics across each era of her five decade journey captured within these pages.

1

Early Life & Education

(1970-1987)

On August 26, 1970, Melissa Ann McCarthy was born in Plainfield, Illinois to Sandra and Michael McCarthy. She was raised on a picturesque 70 acre farm located in a rural corner of the state alongside her sister JoAnn. Life was idyllic during Melissa's early years spent frolicking outdoors, playing make-believe games and showing a goofy, outgoing personality even as a toddler. But tragedy struck suddenly when her cousin and close childhood playmate Jenny died in a horrific car crash at age 8. Melissa struggled coping with the brutal loss of her young best friend, turning inward for months as she grappled with intense grief, fear and uncertainty during her first direct experience with death.

Finally coaxed back into activities by her sympathetic but pragmatic father, Michael used farming as therapy to teach Melissa invaluable lifelong lessons on the realities of life and nature when young calves were born, matured yet also periodically got sick. She learned to accept birth and deaths were inevitable parts of existence. Though still shaken, Melissa's spirits gradually rebounded thanks to the dependable support structure provided by tightly-knit family. Both Sandra and Michael were well-liked, funny individuals themselves as Melissa observed their daily conversational banter filled inside jokes. The McCarthy parents created a nurturing household environment to help guide their daughters through childhood. While Melissa always maintained a slightly anxious edge gained from the tragedy, she regained her outward enthusiasm by age 10 as the family relocated west to join relatives in Boulder, Colorado briefly prior to settling down in the Chicago area suburb of Plainfield for junior high.

Melissa endured predictable awkward early teen years as she entered North Junior High School self-conscious about her body image and self-esteem. She struggled accepting herself as an extremely emotional, sensitive soul who felt things deeply. Melissa grappled with weight even at young age and was taller than classmates, making her an easy target for teasing and questioning her femininity. The increasingly obvious beauty standards of early adolescence triggered lingering doubts. She vented frustrations through overeating tendencies picked up at home where hearty Irish/Catholic comfort cuisine was part of McCarthy family DNA. Unsure how to healthily process nagging insecurities, Melissa compensated outwardly by becoming the "life of the party" - boisterous and fun-loving to camouflage discomfort.

By high school, Melissa's personality adapted in response to teenage angst. She intentionally tried gaining peers' acceptance using humor as means to ingratiate herself with various school social circles from artsy creatives to preppy J.V jocks in hopes of being "cool" by association. Her quick wit and lack of verbal filter amused classmates who appreciated McCarthy's bold candor about touchy topics other shy teens avoided. Yet she felt partially inhibited from showing deepest self to most classmates. Melissa often privately questioned if so-called friends genuinely liked her personally or just enjoyed being entertained by the "class clown" antics. Only in drama club among fellow theater enthusiasts did she feel free expressing range of sentiments to explore her artistic instincts without fear of ridicule.

After barely passing sophomore year while prioritizing fun over academics, mentors helped awaken McCarthy's latent discipline and maturity. She committed focusing efforts productively the next 2 years. Melissa specifically found refuge in school plays under director Sister Beatrice, the teacher who profoundly impacted life by recognizing untapped potential. McCarthy considers the conservative nun among her earliest career cheerleaders for taking Notice of both comedic timing and capability delivering nuanced dramatic performances when given opportunity. Melissa took pride spearheading technically complex productions as assistant director/tech crew head, mastering behind the scenes intricacies like lighting design and stage logistics while honing acting chops performing hilarious sketches or deeply emotional scenes from renowned plays like Death of A Salesman.

By senior year Melissa achieved academic honors, displayed virtuoso range on theater boards and found firmer grounding after years feeling adrift amidst turbulent adolescence. Her artistic passion flourished under supportive Saint Francis Academy environment. Though McCarthy didn't quite fit the slim figures of leading ladies, she landed lead comedic role as the man-crazy Flo Owens in Picnic her senior play thanks to obvious talent. Melissa also served as the school's first female student body president. Just before graduation in 1988, mentors identified special spark that could carry McCarthy far with proper dramatic training. So they assisted securing a prized scholarship spot to study at New York City's prestigious comedy breeding ground - the American Academy of Dramatic Arts. It was a pivotal moment full of optimism. Yet Melissa could hardly imagine the unbelievable adventures which lay ahead as she embarked towards dreams of stardom upon leaving her Illinois home for the Big Apple at just age 18…

2

Early Comedy Career

(1987-1997)

Melissa took an incredible risk venturing to New York City as a small-town 18 year old girl overflowing with ambition but extremely naïve entering show business lion's den in 1987. She tackled cosmetology school by day to financially support herself then rushed to evening acting classes at American Academy of Dramatic Arts, her scholarship spot waiting thanks to suburban Chicago mentors. McCarthy lived in barebones illegal sublets crammed end-to-end with roommates on the rough Lower East Side just trying to survive as she slowly built connections.

Melissa continually faced uphill quest gaining respect as an actress given appearance and style far from leading lady norms. She endured constant industry typecasting for goofy sidekick roles or token fat friend due to her full figure. Most insiders bluntly deemed Melissa lacked the "right" looks regardless of talent. Undeterred, McCarthy took minor parts gravitating towards sketch comedy and improv troupes more accepting of unconventional performers. Early standup gigs at downtown clubs like Stand Up New York tested mettle facing fickle, demanding NYC crowds. She honed observational humor poking fun date mishaps and city living frustrations.

A few small television guest spots followed like playing the cousin of regular character on the sitcom "The Naked Truth". Melissa also landed quirky national commercials needing "funny fat lady", albeit grateful for any paying work. By now she learned dealing with endless audition rejection yet believed versatility could win over remaining skeptics one day. In 1994 Melissa followed boyfriend and fellow struggling performer Ben Falcone who she met in class out West chasing more opportunities in Los Angeles.

The California move marked professional turning point as Melissa finally caught big break at age 24. Wildly popular LA improv group The Groundlings accepted her into their highly competitive training company after intense vetting. Melissa originally feared bombing Groundlings unconventional improvisation courses demanding on-the-spot wit. Instead she thrived unlocking latent talents. Fellow Groundlings members still recall jaw-on-the-floor moments when Melissa's characters and sketches elicited thunderous audience reactions during shows at the cramped 30 seat Groundling Theater. Her previously untapped skill playing multiple outlandish personas helped McCarthy standout from the legendary comedic talent pool emerging there like Will Ferrell, Lisa Kudrow, Phil Hartman and Kristen Wiig.

Melissa parlayed Groundlings clout into increased television and film auditions. Bit parts piled up on shows like Ellen, The Nanny and Jenny McCarthy Show. She landed repeated role as the oddball relative of main characters. Groundlings improv expertise let McCarthy steal scenes vamping dialogue and physical humor. Yet she still found minimal room upward mobility towards mainstream prominence. The consistent typecasting wore Melissa down by late 90s after a decade of paying dues. She pondered leaving acting altogether turning 30 with minimal career advancement, dwindling savings and bi-coastal relationship with Ben struggling despite engagement.

The dispiriting stretch ended unexpectedly when close friend and Academy Award winning actor Shirley MacLaine recommended Melissa for brand new WB comedy-drama series named "Gilmore Girls" in final 2000 casting after reading script pages. Creator Amy Sherman-Palladino envisioned lead character of lovable scatterbrained chef

Sookie St. James perfectly matching Melissa's quirky essence after audition. At first Melissa hesitated risking limited financial security for uncertainty hitting primetime lottery. But at Ben and her family's urging, she took the fateful leap of faith. Almost instantly, Gilmore Girls sparked astonishing resonance with widespread viewership addicted to clever multi-generational plotlines and McCarthy's hilarious performance. Melissa became integral fabric of the show. Sookie garnered her first ever Emmy nomination and vaulted McCarthy into stratosphere just as the 2000s dawned. Little did she realize that playing this wacky sidekick was merely the initial glimpse towards Melisa's forthcoming greatness destined through legendary status…

The pages ahead chronicle the unprecedented ascent still to come.

3

Television Breakthrough

(1997–2010)

Melissa McCarthy's career transformed virtually overnight thanks to her eccentric, animated role as Sookie St. James on "Gilmore Girls". Though initially hired as a secondary character, viewers instantly connected with Melissa's natural rapport opposite stars Lauren Graham and Alexis Bledel by the 2000 season premiere. Her previously untapped talent for longform character development meshed beautifully with creator Amy Sherman-Palladino's idiosyncratic, fast-paced writing style full of pop culture references.

As buzz built, the show leaned heavily into relationship between Graham's Lorelai and Sookie, best friends who co-owned a charming small town Connecticut inn. Their onscreen chemistry resonated hugely with audiences. Melissa rose to challenge matching esteemed dramatic actress Graham punchline for punchline, earning fame for lengthy improvised cooking scenes debating ingredients or freaking out over disorganized kitchens. Though playing a supporting part, funny, optimistic Sookie received comparable fan mail and media queries to the Gilmore leads by sophomore year while carrying several plotlines herself including romance with Jackson Douglas that humanized character beyond just comic relief.

By 2006, Melissa landed among magazine covers and major talk shows discussing Gilmore phenomena entering seventh season still cresting viewership highs unheard of so deep into series run. She took pride seeing once insecure, overweight teenager from suburban Illinois now embraced nationally thanks to highlight role on beloved program. After years struggling on fringes of entertainment industry, Melissa relished accepted place within pop culture zeitgeist. Financial success also finally granted comforts absent during her nomadic early days chasing fame. She purchased first home settling into domestic family life with now husband, Ben Falcone, whom Melissa married shortly after Gilmore pilot episode filmed.

Professionally, new avenues opened for McCarthy to headline additional network television projects during Gilmore hiatus periods. She filmed sitcom pilots and starred in self-titled comedy series "The Melissa McCarthy Show" for 13 episodes alongside veteran actors like Beth Grant. Unfortunately most concepts never got picked up long-term. Industry hesitancy remained betting on Melissa carrying full programs herself despite obvious talent. Her identity still largely centered on being the "funny sidekick" rather than leading lady. But through veteran TV director James Burrows, she secured recurring role alongside Matt LeBlanc on hit CBS sitcom "Samntha Who" before returning to reliable Gilmore Girls home base.

All good things eventually close. By 2006 Melissa felt ready spread creative wings further but agreed short final Gilmore Girls season allowing Amy Sherman-Palladino chance provide satisfying closure for loyal decade long viewership. Inspired by golden era passed, Melissa focused energies pitching own original sitcom ideas drawing upon amusing Midwestern upbringing anecdotes. CBS executives gambled greenlighting multi-camera pilot on McCarthy's concept centering everyday working class woman juggling job, marriage and family. After months writing scenes tailored perfectly to her sensibilities, sitcom ultimately named "Mike & Molly" got approved bringing Ben Falcone onboard directing. The 2010 Fall season premiere introduced these instantly lovable characters firstly through Melissa as 4th grade teacher Molly Flynn seeking true love in Overeaters Anonymous circle. Audiences quickly embraced each episode thanks her undeniable relatability depicting Molly's dating foibles and Laugh out loud yet tender moments self-acceptance alongside Billy Gardell's Officer Mike Biggs. Melissa hit creative groove guiding scenes from perspective of average woman viewers rarely witnessed as television protagonists previously, shattering outdated industry misperceptions. Ratings steadily climbed as buzz amplified around McCarthy's starmaking attraction. She landed magazine covers, late night interviews and burgeoning film offers as Emmy Awards nominations piled up. At 40 years old, Melissa cemented position not just as scene stealing performer but multi-dimensional actress able to carry hit properties herself while pouring creative spirit fully into passion projects reflecting her lived experience. All the eclectic jobs, grueling apprenticeship and identity struggles of past seemed destined to prepare McCarthy for well-earned status as funny, empowering feminist icon ready emerge further from supporting player safety nets into blinding Hollywood spotlight soon to come...

4

Film Fame Begins

(2010–2012)

As Melissa McCarthy crossed into her 40s while cementing TV fame through "Mike and Molly" sitcom heights in 2010, a surprise movie opportunity arose showcasing wider range beyond comedy. Acclaimed director Paul Feig envisioned McCarthy starring in female ensemble project titled "Bridesmaids" he co-wrote with Annie Mumolo centering on womanhood themes never tackled in traditional wedding films. Despite no previous lead movie roles, Melissa felt instant kinship reading script about adult friendships, insecurities and overcoming societal expectations - relatable insights mirroring her own journey. She signed on playing Megan Price, the brash, unfiltered member of group.

"Bridesmaids" production process through 2010 bonded Melissa alongside fellow starring actresses Kristin Wiig, Maya Rudolph and Rose Byrne. They encouraged each other embracing fuller selves in every hilarious or heartbreaking scene while portraying complexities of female psyche beyond typical romcom stereotypes. Under Feig's direction, Melissa improvised outlandish one liners matching Megan's IDGAF attitude. Years channeling own anxieties into over the top characters served brilliantly inhabiting this confident foible.

Sneak peak buzz circulating Hollywood executive screening circles generated visceral reactions unlike any previous McCarthy performances witnessed on network television constraints. Euphoric early audience test reactions confirmed team created something groundbreaking. Yet uncertainty loomed whether such atypical R-rated female humor would actually draw mainstream crowds when released summer 2011.

Those questions evaporated instantly as "Bridesmaids" smashed opening weekend taking the #1 box office spot with $26 million earned - the biggest ever debut for comedy. Buoyed by ecstatic critic reviews praising both gut busting outrageous moments alongside tender friendship storylines, Melissa witnessed her film cement blockbuster status as word of mouth swelled ticket sales week after week. "Bridesmaids" soon surpassed $100 million domestically, a monumental achievement for R rated film reversing outdated marketing assumptions. Overseas audiences similarly propelled international grosses past $200 million total.

Having never starred on the silver screen before, Melissa McCarthy unexpectedly became world famous almost overnight thanks to her magnetic, standout showing. Fans mobbed her with marriage proposals on the street. Critics predicted Oscar nominations recognizing her arrival. Melissa initially grappled transitioning abruptly into in-demand A-List Hollywood persona from relatively normal Midwest life after toiling many years entertainment trenches. Regardless, she wholeheartedly embraced responsibility being public face championing project's feminist statement shaking comedy landscape.

McCarthy traveled extensively promoting "Bridesmaids" message of empowerment and self-acceptance to women young and old who connected with characters. Her whirlwind press tour ranged from blockbuster Mexico City premiere to thoughtful panel conversations on female body image. She walked first ever red carpet at renowned Cannes Film Festival. Elite designers clamored dressing Melissa for glamorous appearances. High fashion opportunity marked incredible shift after years relegated only boxy character woman garments on set. Award nominations rolled in confirming McCarthy as hot property, including Breakout

Comedic Star at Critics Choice Awards, Best Supporting Actress consideration for Academy Awards plus multiple others cementing 2011 her decorated coming out party.

By 2012, Melissa reaped fruits of "Bridesmaids" bonanza with huge film offers arriving nonstop at her agent's desk eager replicating success. She filmed three major roles over next year catapulting Melissa into a whirlwind phase entering peak movie stardom....

5

Movie Stardom

(2012-2016)

Bridesmaids Breakout

Riding high off her star-making performance in Bridesmaids, Melissa McCarthy weighed numerous movie offers now seeing her in an entirely new light as a proven box office draw. She strategically charted career path towards roles allowing full range while further smashing female stereotypes that previously typecasted her. McCarthy fully leveraged the clout and fame amassed relatively late in life to pick unique projects. Having struggled for so long in Hollywood trenches, she committed using hard-won platform dedicated towards further pushing boundaries showing women's multifaceted stories onscreen.

Identity Thief Headliner

First up was crime comedy "Identity Thief" released February 2013 pairing Melissa with Jason Bateman as the title's con artist charging up credit card debts under stolen identities. She committed fully to outrageous physical hijinks and banter as Diana, an incognito swindler living large off spoils until victim Sandy confronts her face-to-face. Melissa held nothing back to create most morally corrupt character yet for her filmography countering typecast niceness. Reuniting with "Bridesmaids" director Seth Gordon, both agreed Melissa could amplify a poorly behaved villain without worry given her immense likability. Audiences wholeheartedly agreed as Identity Thief opened #1 its premiere weekend with over $34 million before finishing domestically at $135 million total - nearly matching Melissa's first film in less than half the time confirming audiences would show up specifically seeing her headline vulgar R-rated films.

The Heat Partnership

Immediately Melissa re-teamed with Paul Feig for 2013 smash action buddy comedy "The Heat" portraying a mismatched FBI agent and Boston detective chasing drug dealers. Melissa lashed sardonic zingers left and right playing Detective Shannon Mullins as the fearsome Boston bulldog to Sandra Bullock's straight-laced investigator Ashburn. In another landmark first, The Heat marked initial R-rated female driven comedy passing $100 million at box office while earning critical praise recognizing how the unorthodox law enforcement duo broke genre molds. Melissa took pride showing that women could lead profitable blockbusters without sacrificing authenticity, vulgarity or storylines balancing compelling personal relationships against pure action. She relished incredible on-set improvisational chemistry jousting opposite the Oscar winner Bullock take after hilarious take bouncing Nicolas Cage impressions, dance moves and insult comedy off their esteemed co-lead while advancing Sisterhood solidarity.

Spy Blockbuster

Spy film sendup "Susan Cooper" soon followed for McCarthy in 2015 after initially planning minor supporting character. But director Paul Feig insisted on evolving into perfect showcase tailor-made capitalizing on her special skills. As the CIA analyst thrust unexpectedly into dangerous field missions, McCarthy nailed uproarious juxtaposition bumbling through exotic locales from Rome to Paris despite lacking innate 007 grace, akin to their Midwestern identities triumphing in sophisticated coastal worlds. Spy pulled no punches on blood, bullets and body humor. Yet Melissa maintained hilarious heart throughout even when accidentally stabbing arms or crashing cars thanks her subtle prowess knowing precisely how and when going over the top. Released summer 2015, Spy cemented McCarthy officially as comedy's undisputed queen with $235 million global gross and opening #1...

By 2016, McCarthy ranked not just the highest paid comedienne but the third overall top female box office draw trailing only pop culture phenomena Jennifer Lawrence and Scarlett Johansson after a mere 5 years doing movies full time. Her unprecedented run generated over $650 million just for studios and climbing fast. Melissa McCarthy officially dominated Hollywood thanks redefining possibilities for funny leading ladies shattering outdated industry misconceptions, to trailblazing feminist feats showing range and relatability capturing loyal audiences globally. Powered by authentic personality channeling real life women's triumphs and insecurities instead of artificial tropes, McCarthy controlled her soaring career trajectory with more barriers to conquer on the horizon...

6

Dramatic Projects and Acclaim

(2016-2020)

Embracing Dramatic Turns

Shortly after Melissa McCarthy completed her unprecedented run dominating box office charts, she purposefully sought more serious acting challenges. While still starring in big commercial comedies annually, McCarthy prioritized roles pivoting perception solely as outrageous physical comedian by highlighting dramatic depth with nuanced indie films garnering awards consideration. She relished surprising doubters, akin to defiance from early career.

Can You Ever Forgive Me? praised McCarthy's dramatic acting prowess to new heights portraying eccentric literary forger Lee Israel opposite Richard E. Grant. She fully embodied the caustic, isolated biographer forced turning to crime selling forged celebrity letters just struggling pay bills.

McCarthy disappearing completely beneath curly hair, thick glasses and biting cynical edge garnering incredible attention as revelation showcasing darker side of human nature yet evoking empathy. Can You Ever Forgive Me? premiered rapturous festival reviews clamoring for Oscar. Despite box office under $10 million, McCarthy won overwhelming Best Actress nominations from Golden Globes, BAFTAs and Critics Choice while taking numerous critics group's top acting honors. Her Academy Award nomination marked first ever recognizing comedy performer in a serious film.

The Kitchen mob drama

In stark departure from signature comedic style, McCarthy joined Tiffany Haddish and Elisabeth Moss leading crime thriller "The Kitchen" portraying a trio of mob wives taking over organized crime operations set in 1970s Hell's Kitchen. Adapting from popular graphic novel, the film envisioned complex descent into underworld violence after husbands get arrested. Melissa leaning full anti-hero in intimidating enforcer role protecting their illicit business turf by any means necessary. Though unfortunately losing box office momentum struggling tone between harsh action and nuanced social commentary, McCarthy relished testing range further on big budget crime noir.

Between serious acting explorations like The Kitchen or Can You Ever Forgive Me?, McCarthy never lost connection with her loyal comedy fans in theaters either..

Life of the Party return to comedy

While spreading dramatic wings, McCarthy simultaneously headlined crowd-pleasing blockbuster comedies annually upholding expert funnywoman title. Hardly missing beat, she wrote slapstick campus laugher Life of The Party imagining a middle aged mom joining college party scene alongside own daughter suddenly becoming classmates. Released May 2018, McCarthy indulged goofy antics dominating beer pong games and joining sorority hijinks like sliding down banisters as nobody's dorm mate pulls uncool mom shenanigans. Though not matching early 2010's sky high numbers, McCarthy's loyal audience showed up yet again earning solid $70 million continuing remarkable longevity selling out multiplexes 13 years into movie stardom.

Thematic culmination in Thunder Force

McCarthy circled back to longtime creative partner Ben Falcone to co-write 2021's female friendship action movie "Thunder Force" imagining super powered outcasts defending Chicago against an evil society. It became a comprehensive culmination of McCarthy's career ethos fighting stigmas by embracing outcasts and celebrating heroes defying impossible physical ideals. As an ordinary woman gaining invisibility superpower alongside childhood BFF Octavia Spencer's newfound indestructibility, Thunder Force unapologetically celebrated comic book absurdity through a female lens with heavy improvisational banter reminiscent of early 2000s McCarthy daring days. Though garnering mixed reviews, the Netflix exclusive reached #1 further displaying Melissa's appeal spanning multiple eras.

After years being undervalued by Tinseltown overly fixated on superficial looks over talent, Melissa McCarthy leveraged immense fame decisively deconstructing bias. Whether dominating Broadway revenuers showcasing comedy chops, earning prestige chasing serious actress accolades or flexing production muscle behind the camera on passion projects, McCarthy continually subverted shallow expectations. She would further stretch creative bounds in the decade ahead wielding power onscreen and off while always uplifting others with inclusive opportunities…

7

Production Roles and Business Ventures

Fashion Label Trailblazer

Amidst her acting workload, Melissa McCarthy proactively launched inclusive women's clothing brand named Seven7 in 2015 embodying confidence beyond sample sizes. Frustrated by lack of fashion-forward options for most real world shapes excluded from beauty standards, she founded company promoting self acceptance at any physique.

McCarthy was all too familiar with wardrobe departments endlessly struggling covering curvier bodies over long career playing roles reflecting average viewers rarely depicted on screen accurately. Determined filling style void herself, Melissa collaborated closely on Seven7 designs focusing meticulous detail towards fit, comfort and quality rather than chasing trends. The debut line offered versatile pieces effortlessly dressed up or down like curve-contouring jeans, sophisticated blouses cut generously and colorful shift dresses in breathable fabrics ideal for women constantly moving between work, home and social commitments.

While niche brands catered higher price plus-sizes, McCarthy priced Seven7 accessibly capturing majority shopper often overlooked entirely by mainstream retailers obsessed with tall, thin mannequins. She made numerous talk show stops proudly wearing her own label highlighting functional details accommodating fuller busts, hips and sleeves without compromising attitude or appeal. Directly addressing the women feeling excluded elsewhere due to weight, McCarthy struck an immediate kinship seeing emotional reactions finally finding current styles celebrating their beauty. Within months, Seven7 expanded aggressively into new categories like swimsuits and denim meeting incredible demand rarely explored for heavier women outside big box "mother of the bride" selections.

Equally fulfilling creatively amidst hectic acting slate, McCarthy gradually assumed full design/marketing leadership duties moving headquarters closer to home. Hands-on attention perfecting back zippers so they don't snag or using high grade flexible denim preventing uncomfortable gapping, Seven7 clothing spoke volumes staying power becoming a staple brand filling wide open niche. Soon annual collections released at New York Fashion Week itself to splashy reception. By keeping costs reasonable despite overnight success, within 4 years Seven7 exceeded eight figure revenues enabling Melissa launch accompanying accessories, jewelry and home décor collections sharing body positive ethos.

On The Day Productions

After years serving loyally under other producers, directors and studios, McCarthy formally announced self-financed production shingle "On The Day" in 2015 as well taking creative reins on passion projects. The company name derived from Melissa's firm belief that effectively preparing allows seamlessly rising occasion facing unpredictable situations - akin to her own circuitous journey towards stardom. Early On The Day projects centered producing husband Ben Falcone's quirky films like "Tammy" letting her develop bigger scale ideas eventually blossoming into vehicles fully showcasing Melissa's sensibilities.

First up was 2016 mother/daughter dramedy Life Of The Party imagining McCarthy matriculating college alongside stunned sorority daughter. Co-writing the script with Falcone, Melissa indulged wicked improv skills opposite young actresses letting veteran chops energize next generation. Though middling reviews criticized generic story, McCarthy's loyal audiences showed up reliably opening at #2 pulling best box office numbers since early 2010s hits. Prolific momentum swiftly followed as On The Day hammered out production/release schedule rivaling actors half her age. Can You Ever Forgive Me? dramatics shot, Chamberlain Heights multicultural cartoon voiced and Nobodies sitcom guest starred within 18 months displaying Melissa's impossibly prolific pace juggling screenwriting, physical comedy shoots and prestige post-production simultaneously like a cinematic Swiss Army knife.

Entering the 2020s with fortunes soaring, McCarthy & Falcone envisioned an expansive slate creating opportunities for wider communities historically struggling visibility in Hollywood and beyond…

Amplifying Underrepresented Voices

On The Day productions strategically focused uplifting diverse voices, beginning with 2019 coming-of-age drama "The Kitchen" alongside Tiffany Haddish and Elisabeth Moss depicting mob wives seizing organized crime power themselves. McCarthy eagerly tackled the enforcer role intimidating rivals in the gritty dramatic thriller adapted from popular graphic novel. Beyond strong performances, behind the scenes Melissa actively mentored rookie filmmakers especially women/people of color in key creative roles as Directors, Cinematographers and Production Designers gaining invaluable training often barred Hollywood's notorious old boy's network.

McCarthy further leaned into producing family friendly stories reflecting her core values like 2019's "The Starling" nurturing grief through quirky metaphor. She portrayed a grieving mother finding symbolic hope when forced co-parent orphaned baby bird alongside frustrated husband Kevin Kline. The tender Netflix drama spotlighted real emotional dynamics after devastating loss especially for couples struggling intimacy post-trauma. Award winning television director Theodore Melfi praised On The Day championing his cinematic vision and pushing boundaries showing raw vulnerability between older onscreen partners. More reflective passion projects followed highlighting untold stories - from HBO Max's "Nine Perfect Strangers" wellness satire to 20th Television sitcom "God's Favorite Idiot" co-starring husband Ben Falcone as modern day Clark Kent.

Through strategic producing power moves on her own terms, Melissa McCarthy simultaneously fostered entertainment opportunities for others while further cementing formidable Hollywood legacy beyond merely starring fame. Rainmaker clout opened doors enabling creative risks traditional studio structures balked. Whether casting unknown talents or securing financing telling unconventional stories, McCarthy's production banner made seismic impact just entering its second decade birthing original content. She mapped blueprint path forward for peers in the fickle aging actress era by proactively building self-sustaining independent studio model, ultimately preparing McCarthy tackle directing herself when the time felt right.

8

Awards and Achievements

Primetime Emmy Acclaim

Melissa McCarthy received her biggest acting accolades on the television screen including multiple Emmy Award nominations and wins cementing small screen dominance nearly matching film success. Her hilarious performances kept audiences in stitches for 20 years evolving characters weekly tapping endless comedic wells.

McCarthy's earned first ever Emmy nomination for Outstanding Supporting Actress playing lovable chef Sookie St. James on pop culture phenomenon "Gilmore Girls" through early 2000s. Though not victorious, the attention validated McCarthy as integral ingredient keeping viewers passionately engaged returning episode after episode.

Once McCarthy starred carrying her own sitcom creation "Mike and Molly", trophy hardware quickly followed thanks undeniable lead actress chemistry opposite Billy Gardell. Melissa landed Outstanding Lead Actress in a Comedy Series nod each season between 2011 and 2015 including back-to-back Emmy night wins in 2011 and 2012. The consecutive victories marked rare achievement for a broadcast network comedy performer among cable/streaming program juggernauts. Beyond trophies, "Mike and Molly" further showcased McCarthy's writing/production chops adapting real world experiences into accessible humor about average working folks.

In all, Melissa McCarthy accumulated 5 Emmy acting nominations over a decade playing two beloved television characters etching permanent pop culture influence.

Big Screen Recognition

Though lacking major competitive film awards, McCarthy's consistent box office dominance and audience admiration accounted for immense Hollywood influence regardless. Her unprecedented late career explosion generating nearly $700 million in ticket sales by 2016 marked all-time record smashing various "first ever female" benchmarks. Already the first woman spearhead $35 million+ comedy opening with The Heat, Melissa became first female lead crossing

$200 million global twice consecutively with Tammy then Spy.

Such meteoric commercial success sparked immediate mainstream fame and magazine covers. Prestigious institutions like Time Magazine named McCarthy one of the "100 Most Influential People" in 2016 for spearheading female-driven projects and representing empowering messages. Despite no Oscar or Globe victories herself, McCarthy did land Critics' Choice Film Best Actress nods for both comedies (The Heat) and dramatic work (Can You Ever Forgive Me?).

Underscoring Melissa's pop culture imprint, she earned star on the iconic Hollywood Walk of Fame in 2015 barely 5 years into big screen career. For an actress lacking typical ingenue looks, the swift commemorative honor so early signaled fierce impact conquering dated Tinseltown stereotypes. It took legends like Julia Roberts or Tom Hanks over a decade commanding similar spotlight. Despite film academy snubs, McCarthy earned status as a marquee name selling out theaters globally identified by first name alone.

Comedy Trailblazer Recognition

In addition to McCarthy's individual Emmy and box office feats, she received countless honors for trailblazing work elevating female-led comedies into mainstream prominence over historically male dominated landscape.

Major Hollywood institutions took notice as McCarthy continually selected bold projects spotlighting empowering yet hilariously flawed women. From the raunchy Bridesmaids ensemble to The Heat buddy cop subversion, McCarthy films pushed R-rated boundaries earning critical raves recognizing razor sharp improvisational talents.

Both elite professional groups like the Broadcast Film Critics Association and niche comedy collectives lauded her innovation. McCarthy won "Comedy Star of the Year" and "Comedy Actress" awards from Critics Choice, MTV Movie Awards, Hollywood Film Festival and other ceremonies through early 2010s. Variety Magazine, Rolling Stone and virtually every entertainment press outlet prominently featured McCarthy for pioneering status as few women dared profane big screen comedy previously.

Even competing actresses publiclySingled out McCarthy's courage advancing opportunities. Oscar winner Jennifer Lawrence wrote letters crediting McCarthy's vulgar, carefree comedic roles empowering younger cohort expanding creative options beyond just dramas or family films. Established legends like Shirley Maclaine emerged one of McCarthy's earliest high profile supporters fighting for initial acting chances on Gilmore Girls pilot.

While shrugging off "trailblazer" labels herself, McCarthy always voiced deep appreciation towards fellow creatives recognizing difficult journey faced. Her Six Seven clothing brand and productions centered opening doors so more marginalized communities get opportunities going forward. Through it all, the comedian stays firmly grounded in midwestern roots even enjoying A-list fame.

In summary, McCarthy racked both television's highest comedy acting trophies plus cemented status as a elite box office attraction through genuine personality resonating way beyond physical appearance. Her influence shattered glass ceilings opening doors towards more representation.

9

Balancing Career and Family

Midwest Values Grounding Chaotic Hollywood Life

Even while ascending the peak of show business fame, Melissa McCarthy actively nurtured family life raising two daughters with actor-director husband Ben Falcone between blockbuster film shoots and acclaimed television projects through the 2010s. The pair relied on Midwestern grounded values and teamwork balancing hectic schedules under Hollywood spotlight.

Melissa first met fellow struggling performer Falcone in late 1990s performing together at legendary Los Angeles comedy troupe The Groundlings. Their quirky improvisational chemistry clashed instantly birthing sketches stealing the show on tiny 30 seat theater stage. Romance blossomed gradually before marriage in 2005 just as McCarthy landed her career catapulting role on "Gilmore Girls".

Determined keeping private lives grounded amidst major primetime exposure, the couple soon started family away from Hollywood hullabaloo on a quiet ranch outside Los Angeles. Daughter Vivian was born in 2007 with second daughter Georgette following in 2010. While McCarthy's sitcom and movie roles often reflected chaotic matriarchs, she strived being steady calming force focusing home life. Melissa mastered skill slipping mommy persona on hiatus days before effortlessly tapping manic characters when red light flipped on. Motherhood's tender unconditional lens tamed inner critics judging creative instincts.

Falcone frequently appeared on-set when possible both supporting Melissa while gaining behind-camera apprenticeship. The parents tag teamed logistics allowing McCarthy follow acting passions globetrotting wherever movie sets took her. Whether Wisconsin school teacher in Life of The Party or CIA spy turned rogue agent in Spy,

Melissa fully embodied each transformation trusting Ben hold down domestic frontlines at home through his own directing projects. Their carefree candid companionship thrived built upon mutual devotion and laughter.

By mid 2010s, both daughters occasionally featured playing younger McCarthy in flashback scenes letting the girls soak behind the scenes glamour themselves. McCarthy cherished opportunities sharing professional worlds with family firsthand bringing added meaning fulfilling lifelong performer dream. She often laughingly mentions inherit creative "hamminess" coming from kids already comfortable on camera.

Professionally Falcone became integral directing several McCarthy starring vehicles including Tammy, The Boss and Life of The Party comedies. Their seamless shorthand communication style developed through decades sparring improv scenes facilitated smooth movie sets. Melissa felt secure taking outrageous risks bouncing skits off spouse/director fully supporting each other's punchlines while elevating humor echoing their quirky domestic life ridiculousness. Through chaotic moments losing wigs mid-take or wrestling prop malfunctions, McCarthy's boisterous sets fostered warm familial atmosphere thanks to Falcone partnership secured by unshakeable marriage beyond merely transactional careerism.

The ordinary Midwest parents now worth hundreds of millions dollars never lost grounded roots or outsider perspective struggling early years clawing Hollywood footholds step by step together. Their films exude aspirational themes overcoming steep odds ultimately triumphant through self-acceptance - messages organically woven through McCarthy family dynamics in real life too. Melissa continues prioritizing daughters and husband requirements filming locations/schedules allowing everyone chase passions without sacrificing precious memories. After all grounding principles gained young shaped entire journey, McCarthy enters her sixth decade determined upholding Midwest values anchoring chaotic fame whirlwind.

Using Platform to Empower Others

As McCarthy's star rose to iconic fame levels, she and Ben Falcone firmly committed leveraging hard-won influence opening entertainment industry access towards groups historically lacking opportunity.

McCarthy's production company On the Day actively nurtured upcoming female directors, writers and crew gaining invaluable major studio feature experience shadowing veterans. Whether mentoring women cinematographers on The Boss or casting unknown acting talents as Life of the Party sorority sisters, McCarthy enjoyed paying forward crucial breaks she received early on from risk-taking supporters like TV director James Burroughs.

Beyond set life, McCarthy's celebrity profile enabled advocating public stances supporting body positivity and self-acceptance beyond typical Hollywood superficiality. From proudly flaunting curves during Mike and Molly days to launch of her inclusive clothing line, McCarthy turned fame into megaphone championing women feeling marginalized by unfair societal beauty biases. She relished receiving emotional fan letters from overweight viewers finally seeing realistic role models thriving on screen.

During awards speeches and interviews, McCarthy always shifted focus towards creating entertainment reflecting compassion. She cited deep friendships formed through production companies and joke-filled group texts maintaining work/life balance. McCarthy's humility and generosity resonated hugely despite reaching icon status levels.

Passion for nurturing female voices led McCarthy embracing directing debut herself on quirky comedy film Bobbie Sue, anticipated releasing 2023. After observing trusted collaborator Falcone command sets seamlessly, McCarthy felt prepared finally stepping behind camera fully realizing long-term dreams. Though initially intimidated by scale undertaking everything from guiding actors to reviewing editing bays, McCarthy characteristically relied on support systems built over decades in Hollywood to expand skillsets, paying kindness forward for next generation.

10

Continued Prominence and Impact

(2020-present)

Defying Ageism with Consistent Success

Entering her 50s amidst youth-obsessed Hollywood ecosystem skewing younger for desirable female performers, Melissa McCarthy continually secured major box office comedies plus additional dramatic work gaining serious acting admiration over the mid 2020s.

As a rare leading lady headliner past 40, McCarthy scored sizable $100 million total global grosses with a wedding comedy "Superintelligence" and Disney's female-focused superhero romp Thunderforce, each released during height of Covid uncertainty displaying durable appeal. McCarthy lent quirky charm voice acting lead villain for 2021's The Boss

Baby sequel overcoming simultaneous HBOMax streaming release outgrossing original by tens of millions.

Becoming a brand name unto herself over quarter century cementing fame, McCarthy attracted huge sums attached merely announcing projects in development like holiday comedy "Margie Claus". Filmmakers touted Melissa's comedic Midas touch blessing future scripts. Meanwhile 2023 Sundance darling "Bearskin" won raves continuing nuanced dramatic range as war veteran hiding Appalachian wilds opposite Joey King.

Throughout early 2020s, McCarthy's television dominance continued securing scene stealing guest appearances on buzzy sitcoms Leverage: Redemption plus Hulu breakout Only Murders in the Building standing out among much younger ensemble casts. Such extended prime signaled McCarthy's impact anchoring small screen hits across full generation.

Additionally on streaming, McCarthy earned executive producer credit collaborating with Nicole Kidman atop Prime Video nail salon dark comedy "20th Century Girl" further expanding creative prowess directing select episodes herself.

Cultural Influence Extending Beyond Fame Itself

Rather than clinging fame spotlights later years, McCarthy leveraged hard-won industry clout paying opportunities forward uplifting marginalized groups still struggling adequate Hollywood representation both in front and behind cameras. Her production company prioritized female-forward projects like Diane Lane aging actress film "Last Will" tackling ageism. McCarthy also negotiated actively for wider size costuming/wardrobe budgets on sets initiating body positive improvements confronting skinny star norms.

Additionally Melissa expanded lifestyle brands celebrating women beyond fashion with decor, jewelry and beauty accessories lines exuding whimsical confidence. A 2022 home goods partnership with WalMart smashed sales projections immediately connecting McCarthy's appeal average hometown shoppers nationwide.

Acknowledging trail impacted countless aspiring creatives, McCarthy took active mentoring young talents via masterclass workshops and university Q&A visits. She frankly discussed overcoming early career barriers as plus size performer long before mainstream body positivity penetration. McCarthy's authentic vulnerability and humor motivated upcoming generation paying hard lessons forward.

Finally circling towards directing debut herself on 2023 release "Bobbie Sue", McCarthy relied on own extensive rolodex bringing esteemed veterans into fresh project. By proactively opening access, McCarthy organically built supportive community allowing achieving wide dreams imagined scribbling sketches Midwest bedrooms decades prior.

From those imaginative childhood beginnings McCarthy continually nurtured communal opportunities lifting marginalized voices towards realizing their untapped potential too - the ultimate legacy beyond individual fame and fortune lasting generations to come. The final arc of McCarthy's biographical journey sees dreams coming full circle as she graduates confidently center stage directing talents towards creating space for others still struggling margins…much as she once did.

The Comedic Icon's Next Horizon

As Melissa McCarthy enters the sixth decade of an already legendary show business career, the passion for creating laughs and telling representative stories burns brighter than ever.

Shortly after completing her feature film directorial debut on 2023's "Bobbie Sue", McCarthy already has multiple high profile acting projects slated keeping hilarious momentum charging forward. Upcoming roles include starring alongside Nicole Kidman in busy 2023 film slate for Prime Video alongside major studio comedies reuniting frequent McCarthy collaborators like director Ben Falcone.

On the production front, McCarthy and Falcone's On The Day company recently announced series adaptation of 2018 coming-of-age film "Can You Ever Forgive Me?" for Hulu. With McCarthy executive producing alongside lead actress Victoria Clark, the spirited dark comedy will fictionalize further adventures from Lee Israel's real world escapades forging celebrity letters. The series encapsulates McCarthy's ethos embracing complicated female lead characters rarely spotlighted on screen.

Having shattered countless barriers and stereotypes over her trailblazing career, Melissa McCarthy continually leveraged hard won influence to lift up next generation of women and marginalized communities towards their highest potential. All while keeping audiences around the world in stitches for 30 years and counting at the apex of entertainment. This comedy icon's impact reverberates across film, television and culture itself entering the 2030s future as McCarthy writes, produces and directs bold new visions showcasing the multifaceted female experience with plenty still left to say.

11

Conclusion

Melissa McCarthy: Still Breaking Limits

"Melissa McCarthy holds a place in Hollywood history ascending from struggling underdog performer into the top tier of acclaimed multi-faceted entertainment moguls redefining all possibilities for women across the industry built upon decades of authentic enthusiasm and hard work defying the odds each step of the way.

From her humble beginnings growing up inside a typical Midwestern American family far removed from the cultural movers and shakers to ultimately rivaling elite contemporary icons like Jennifer Lawrence or Margot Robbie among popular culture's highest-paid actresses and producing moguls, McCarthy's unlikely biography stands triumphant overcoming so many obstacles continually underestimated for her identity as a plus sized female comedy performer.

Yet over 40 years, never wavering from a grounded perspective in real world daily struggles of real women empowered McCarthy never fit conventional roadmaps to stardom built entirely around slim physical beauty ideals winning the odds instead through sheer willpower, undeniable charisma and wildly inventive comedic chops soon recognized across generations of admiring audiences still adapting fresh projects towards inclusivity and accessibility today.

From childhood gravitating towards creative passion plays and celebrity impersonations, through her teenage jobs in unglamorous Boulder malls barely getting by those early years chasing unlikely performance dreams out West, to the next brutally long decade toiling Los Angeles improv comedy trenches facing constant typecasting bias as the token "fat funny friend", McCarthy's journey feels ripe for underdog silver screen storytelling itself one day.

Even her first taste of stability playing kooky chef Sookie St James on the 2000s touchstone Gilmore Girls felt merely prelude towards seismic superstardom soon to come. After years paying dues from television bit parts to off Broadway theaters and emerging alternative comedy platforms welcoming oddball personas, McCarthy at long last exploded onto the worldwide scene thanks breakout film role in

Bridesmaids. That landmark ensemble heralded a renaissance showing women leading R-rated blockbusters previously unfathomable in sexist studio climates.

Instantly McCarthy seized hard fought spotlight levers herself into Hollywood's elite upper echelon through relentless output staying busy nearly every year since. Whether physically demanding slapstick roles falling down college steps or disappearing dramatically behind prosthetics earning serious actress credentials, McCarthy continually subverted limitations others projected onto plus sized talents creatively thriving into her 50s where most female thespians watch opportunities dwindle fighting ageism.

Beyond just on camera brilliance, McCarthy simultaneously ascended upper industry tiers writing scripts, producing series uplifting marginalized voices, launching clothing empires celebrating fuller female bodies, even directing upcoming passion projects focused empowering women supporting others scale the system just as she persevered. That behind the scenes clout lets McCarthy shepherd new generations carrying messages of radical self-acceptance against unrealistic media ideals.

Now 30 years since arriving Los Angeles with $58 total savings but overflowing hopes to somehow connect comedic gifts just yearning expression against odds through tearful weeks desperately lonely, Melissa McCarthy stands triumphant as living rebuttal that mentors words echoing still... "Just wait until you get opportunity show what you can fully do".

Well the world happily witnessed exactly the glorious heights McCarthy could achieve thanks forging her own opportunities then elevating others along with her. The young girl from Plainfield now fittingly takes rightful place beside more conventionally marketed luminaries among the definitive entertainment icons from Hollywood's initial hundred plus years.

Yet McCarthy's cultural influence stretches well beyond fame itself as the loads of young misfits may lack her name recognition but recognize pieces themselves within the self-described "weird chick" proudly flying own freak flags towards Purpose and dreams barely imaginable by outside voices seeking to define worth through restrictive checklists.

Likewise the women of all backgrounds who shed tears finally feeling visible for the first time or gained confidence being exactly who God created no matter shape or form seeing McCarthy defiantly become America's sweetheart blazing new trails thriving entirely on own terms gives hope lasting lifetimes.

As this book traces through the many biographical inflection points across five decades rising improbable celebrity pantheon through determination and mass appeal, McCarthy's serialized memoirs would remain incomplete herself still chasing so much undiscovered horizons ahead. Approaching just her sixth decade living, Melissa McCarthy's unlikely success story refuses slowing down continuing prove limitless talents beyond token stereotypes.

The closing passage of McCarthy's biography thus signals not a conclusion but celebratory comma towards whatever she manifests further now speaking, writing, producing and directing fully self actualized voice towards the world. May we all learn from McCarthy's conviction pursuing creativity against doubts in order to lift up communities allowing every beautiful square peg finally fit belonging without self-judgement.

Just as a mid 20th century adage once promised... 'You ain't seen nothing yet'. When it comes to the endless possibility of Melissa McCarthy's magical entertainment gifts, truer words may never apply more fittingly".

Afterword

APPENDIX

Melissa McCarthy Awards and Nominations

Television:

Emmy Awards:
 - 2011: Won - Outstanding Lead Actress in a Comedy Series - Mike & Molly
 - 2012: Won - Outstanding Lead Actress in a Comedy Series - Mike & Molly
 - 2013: Nominated - Outstanding Lead Actress in a Comedy Series - Mike & Molly
 - 2014: Nominated - Outstanding Lead Actress in a Comedy Series - Mike & Molly
 - 2015: Nominated - Outstanding Lead Actress in a Comedy Series - Mike & Molly

Critics Choice TV Awards:
- 2011: Nominated - Best Actress in a Comedy Series - Mike & Molly
- 2012: Won - Best Actress in a Comedy Series - Mike & Molly

TCA Awards:
- 2011: Nominated - Individual Achievement in Comedy - Mike and Molly

Satellite Awards:
- 2020: Nominated - Best Actress in a Supporting Role in a Musical-Comedy or Drama Television Series - Nine Perfect Strangers

Film:

Academy Awards:
- 2019: Nominated - Best Actress - Can You Ever Forgive Me?

BAFTA Awards:
- 2019: Nominated - Best Actress in a Leading Role - Can You Ever Forgive Me?

Critics Choice Movie Awards:
- 2012: Nominated - Best Comedy Actress - Bridesmaids
- 2012: Nominated - Best Comedy Actress - Bridesmaids
- 2014: Nominated - Best Actress in a Comedy - The Heat
- 2014: Nominated - Best Actress in a Comedy - Tammy
- 2018: Nominated - Best Actress - Can You Ever Forgive Me?

MTV Awards:
- 2012: Won - Best Comedic Performance - Bridesmaids

People's Choice Awards:
- 2014: Nominated - Favorite Comedic Movie Actress
- 2015: Nominated - Favorite Comedic Movie Actress
- 2016: Nominated - Favorite Comedic Movie Actress

Teen Choice Awards:
- 2013: Nominated - Choice Movie Actress: Female - The Heat
- 2014: Nominated - Choice Movie Actress: Comedy - Tammy
- 2016: Won - Choice Movie Actress: Comedy - Spy

Made in the USA
Monee, IL
09 August 2024